A Step, a Stroll
A Blog, a Book

Collecting My Thoughts

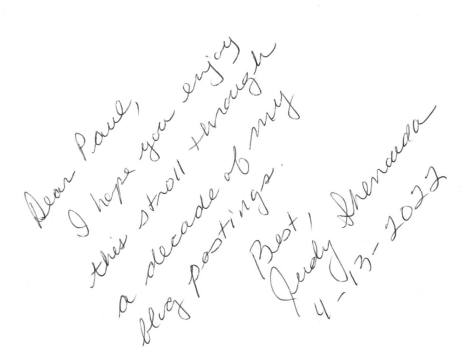

Dear Paul,
I hope you enjoy
this stroll through
a decade of my
blog postings.

Best, Shenauda
Judy Shenauda
4-13-2022

A Step, a Stroll
A Blog, a Book

Collecting My Thoughts

Judith Ellison Shenouda

Shenouda Associates Inc.
Pittsford, NY

Copyright © 2022 Judith Ellison Shenouda

Creative design and editorial services by Shenouda Associates Inc. Pittsford, NY, USA

ISBN 13: 978-1-7322223-6-6

ISBN 10: 1-7322223-6-6

Contents

Dedication 4

Acknowledgments 4

Preface 5

Calendar 6

Take a First Step. Let the Momentum Unfold. 7

Advice Can Be Your Valentine's Day Gift 9

Stops and Starts 11

Organization, Organization, Organization—
There's More than A to Z 14

Time to Lighten Up 18

'Tis the Season… 23

A Team to Pull Your Sleigh 26

Wellness and Happiness—As Easy as ABC 29

Writing 31

Wood Works Wonders 32

Audiences Might Like to Know… 34

Pour Patterns, Thoughts, Connections,
and Ideas onto Paper 38

It Takes an Acrobat to Organize Content 40

Inspire Thyself 44

The eLearning Companion to Career Success
in 12 Easy Steps: A Journal 47

I Helped You. I Received My Reward.
The Score Is Even. 50

Sweeten Your Days 52

Business..55

My Job: Taking Care of Business 56

Conference Notes 59

Your Goods Have Value 61

I Am Unique and So Are You. We Are Keepers. 64

How Does Your Garden Grow?......................66

Do for Others, and Have Others Do for You...............68

Hurray for You...70

Yin and Yang—You Can Do a Balancing Act 72

Communities 74

Good Communities—Make Them Happen 75

Afformations—Forms that Say Yes 78

Reading Nonfiction Books 80

Reading Nonfiction Books Continued 85

Book Club Prep..88

Passages 92

Gratitude. Generosity. Sustenance........................93

A Granddaughter Remembers.....................96

Give Away that Which You Hope to Receive.............100

Dear One 102

I'll See You Again 104

Her Company **106**

    About Us 107

Closing **113**

Notes **114**

Dedication

A Step, a Stroll, a Blog, a Book: Collecting My Thoughts is dedicated to those who are ready, willing, and able to take one step, take another, create momentum, make progress, and transform what is into what can be.

Acknowledgments

Applying their knowledge of design principles, mastery of publishing tools, many talents, and even brilliance, those with whom I work at Shenouda Associates Inc. helped shape and form this book, my earlier books, and the many business and technical guides, manuals, and deliverables created for our clients. I acknowledge, admire, and thank them for their enormous contributions.

Preface

From March 2020 to today—the final weeks of December 2021—sheltering in place has become commonplace, courtesy of an unwelcome guest's arrival on the global scene. Client work creating technical and business publications has been ongoing, but time spent going to and from work sites, attending meetings, and participating in conferences has waned.

With the gift of time came opportunities to explore new tools and create new products. *A Step, a Stroll, a Blog, a Book: Collecting My Thoughts* is the result of one employee's desire to learn Jutoh to create an eBook without first creating a print book. Learn it, he did. Another employee with a keen eye helped with the cover design.

We used a decade of my blog postings as the content. It quickly became apparent that postings written from 2011 through 2021 could not be used as is. Thus, I grouped, organized, and edited them to make a readable book.

May you be enriched learning about my books, my business, and those who make it possible.

Judith Ellison Shenouda

Calendar

Take a First Step.
Let the Momentum Unfold.

Blog posting January 15, 2014

Sometimes, we look at the end result of a new endeavor and get stuck. The effort needed to start and the energy required to persist are just too much. So, what can we do? We can take a first step. We can take a second step and a third.

I recall hearing a new year's resolution a while ago, in which someone wanted to start an exercise routine. She committed to taking this one step every day— after getting dressed, she would put on her running shoes. The next thing she knew, she was outdoors every day and walking. As the days wore on, she picked up her pace, making good use of those running shoes.

For all of us, in time, the momentum builds, and the results become apparent. Making progress and achieving a goal no longer seem difficult or insurmountable. I took a first step a few months ago on a family project.

While wishing my cousin well on upcoming surgery, I heard the worry in her voice. To get onto a more upbeat topic, I asked this wonderful cook and baker for some favorite family recipes. Next thing I heard was, "We should get these recipes into a family cookbook." We both agreed on step one. Since she would now have the gift of time, she would send an email to all the cousins, asking them to send her some favorite recipes. I was copied in on the responses.

As a wise person once said, "Be careful what you wish for." Not only did we receive recipes, we received requests for recipes—Grandma Gert's rice pudding; Aunt Jeanette's sour cream, chocolate cake; and Cousin Mac's cream cheese and pineapple brownies. And we heard some amusing family lore. Syd overturned Grandma's big pot of fish that was slowly cooking atop the stove, and, sweet as she was, Grandma simply started the laborious process over again. Rhoda filled customers' requests for a banana split at the soda fountain in her dad's drug store by quietly going lickity-split out the back door to buy the requisite bananas. Grandma's mile-high lemon meringue pie and other cooking delights helped to win the heart of her daughter's beau.

One hundred plus pages later, this project is well past step one and has taken on a life of its own. Those who remember the sights, tastes, and aromas of the older generations' kitchens are keeping them alive for the younger generations and generations to come. By summer, we will have a cookbook—a family treasure—and a wonderful reason to congregate.

What first steps have you taken that produced surprisingly happy results? We'd love to hear.

Update

The finished book, *A Bisl of This, A Bisl of That: Eating Our Way*, is now available in print and eBook versions.

Advice Can Be Your Valentine's Day Gift

Blog posting February 13, 2013

It is said that advice is cheap. We know that many people give it freely. So freely, that those of us on the receiving end often pay little attention. Since this month includes Valentine's Day, I started thinking about how advice is sometimes a precious gift. Let me introduce you to Thomas Transport, Star Singer, and Polly Politico. Consider how their advice can inspire you to dream about your career success, give you high hopes, and motivate you to take some next steps.

Like Orville and Wilbur Wright, Thomas Transport is an inventor. He dreams of combining technologies from land, sea, and air transports into a brand new vehicle. Some say that Thomas's new vehicle can't be built, because the design he envisions has never been built before. Yet, he continues to tinker with the many scrap parts he collects from builders of traditional modes of transportation. He persists. His advice? Keep at it. Accept others' discards. Experiment. You might just transform what appears to be junk into a real treasure.

Star Singer lost her job and her home. Yet, she continues to dream that someday, one of those homes she sees with a "for sale" sign will be her home. As she looks at the smoke coming from a chimney, she envisions a day when she will be warmly snuggled inside. Though hungry, Star finds it difficult to ask for help. The solution? She volunteers to work in a community cupboard as payment for food. She sees others with needs, offers a smile and a song, starts entertaining for free, and then finds paid gigs. One day, she will have a home and fill a community cupboard for others. Star's advice? Whatever your current circumstance, pick up the pieces, start over, and remember to give back.

Polly Politico dreams of one day being President. Still in her 20s, she runs for mayor of her town and dreams of empowering all constituents—young, old, disenfranchised, and privileged—to revitalize the community. Polly's campaign has its challenges. The naysayers claim, "You're too young. You never ran for public office before. You have no political experience. Who would vote for you?" Yet, Polly does not listen. With her promotional flyers in hand, she campaigns door to door, attends events, and involves everyone she knows in her innovative fundraisers. The media become interested in her style and in her substance. The more people see and hear of Polly, the more they like her. Outfinanced, Polly, in fact, loses this election, but she will run again. Her advice? "Win or lose, keep on keeping on."

Consider this advice from Thomas, Star, and Polly. When it comes to your career success, have a dream, and have high hopes that you can make it happen. Find ways to remove, erase, delete, go around, go under, go over, go through, or transform any obstacle. Make the obstacle small. Frame it as a minor inconvenience, a mere irritation, a challenge, an opportunity. May this advice be a welcome Valentine's Day gift as you take the next steps to your career success.

Stops and Starts

Blog posting March 25, 2015

Nature is filled with stops and starts that just happen, without any effort or coaxing from human beings. We see that the snow that covered the ground for months is almost gone, giving way to soggy soil and brown, slightly green grass. We hear the songs of robins and see crocuses popping through the earth. We listen, we watch, we shed our armor of heavy coat, hat, gloves, and boots and greet a new season. If only our work life stopped and started so naturally. If only we could recharge by pressing a magic button. My work world—and maybe yours, too—is filled with projects, where an element of angst accompanies the stops and the starts and, at times, the phases in between.

Stops

I now see the finish line approaching on one book project that has occupied my mind and energy for several months. The client is reviewing a draft that I will then tweak, as needed, and prepare for publication. It seems that the difficult work of transforming lots of content into an organized, readable, interesting book is almost ready to stop. There are some signs that this work, like the robin and the crocus, will sing and bloom. I will watch as this book project leaves me and takes on a life of its own.

Starts

While my efforts on one book project are about to stop, I hem and haw about a new project that is about to start. Unlike the start of spring that, sooner or later, just happens, this new assignment, which is a chapter in a book that will have many contributors, is not miraculously taking shape. No, it needs some prodding, some cajoling, some poking around. Since this new book is a collection, there is already a theme to consider. Yet, what I want to convey in my chapter is vague. How and where do I begin?

The magic button

I look at the almost-done book project that months ago also had a start. Many centuries ago, a victorious Julius Caesar said, "I came, I saw, I conquered." I now say, "I started. I persevered. I finished." Knowing that I have succeeded before in moving from a blank page to a book in hand, I know that I can do it again and, optimistically, again and again. By summer or fall, I have every reason to believe that I will have my chapter written, reviewed, and ready for publication. I am ready to press the magic "Start" button and do what I can to create some momentum.

Your thoughts

Do projects that have stopped because your role is complete and the work product is ready to move from your hands into someone else's hands help fuel the start of your new projects? Do you have special, tried-and-true ways to approach that new project that is not springing into shape? I would love to hear how you jumpstart that new project that is yet unformed.

Organization, Organization, Organization—There's More than A to Z

Blog posting July 30, 2012

Practicing for our Singalong with Gert

Summer means it's time to prepare Ma's picnic for our extended family and her ever-evolving circle of friends. My role is to compile the list of invitees, send out the invitations, and, most important of all, prepare the handout, *Singalong with Gert.* Recently, I sent her the list of songs we discussed—a combination from previous years and a few new ones. I created the list and sorted it **alphabetically**. That way, I could easily identify and delete duplicate titles from the list. When I sent her the alphabetical list, she did not like the sequence. A singalong should not progress from "Aba Daba Honeymoon" to "Zip-a-Dee-Doo-Dah." Musically, it makes no sense.

Of course, as a good daughter, I went through several revisions, and I think we now have it right. We start with "Hail, Hail, the Gang's all Here." We sprinkle some of the happy, smile songs throughout—"Just Let a Smile be Your Umbrella"; "When You're Smiling";

and "Smile, Darn You, Smile." We made sure that Ma's favorite songs are at the top of the list, since with 50 songs, we may not sing them all. We will, though, conclude with the last song on the list, "May the Good Lord Bless and Keep You." So variety and **importance** factored into the organization.

Getting the sequence right made me think about organization in publications. Whether it's a song list, report, manual, brochure, book, blog, or any other piece, the organization is important to the reader, which means it must be important for the writer. A writer may create a piece using one organizational principle. For example, the writer with a list of topics to cover might have complete information on some topics, small gaps in information on others, and meager information on yet others. It makes sense to write the topics for which the information is most complete and, as the information on other topics gets fleshed out, write those topics. When all topics are written, the writer takes into account the sequence that makes sense for the reader. Here is where there are many options.

Let's say you are writing a brochure that introduces shoppers to the layout of a new supermarket. Organizing your brochure **spatially** might make sense. For example, aisle one includes fruits, vegetables, and beverages; aisle two has meat, seafood, delicatessen, and cheeses; aisle three has soups, canned goods, sauces, spices, and seasonings; and so forth. If your brochure includes a section on shopping for food essentials, you might want to organize the section from **basic to complex**. The basics might include essential items that must appear on your shopping list: proteins, vegetables, carbohydrates, and fats.

You might progress to a more complex section that includes the ready-made meals and elegant pastries that the supermarket offers.

You might be writing a quick start guide to accompany a new desktop computer, monitor, keyboard, and mouse. How do you organize the contents? You likely do so **chronologically**. Step one: Check that you have received all of the items on the packing list. Step two: Unpack all of the components. Step three: Connect the various components. Step four: Check that the computer starts up and that the monitor displays the preloaded software applications. After all is said and done, if all does not work as expected, try the troubleshooting techniques. Since you do not have the space to address every possible item that could go awry, the techniques presented are likely selected based on **frequency** of occurrence.

If you are a financial planner, you might write a paper that educates your clients on your approach to amassing and retaining wealth. You might start by organizing the discussion into **problem and solution**. The problem might be having sufficient funds for your entire life. The solution for achieving that goal can include a number of options related to savings, investments, retirement age, and so forth. Your paper might use **cause and effect** to identify what leads to outliving your resources. Perhaps you will present an argument with the **pros and cons** of various investment strategies. And you likely will **compare and contrast** your philosophy and results with those of your competitors.

In real estate, they talk about location, location, location. In publications, we talk about organization,

organization, organization. What can you add to the organizational principles presented? We're eager to hear from you.

Time to Lighten Up

Blog posting December 31, 2015

Over the Thanksgiving holiday with siblings in the home where I grew up, I was delighted to see the beautiful cypress bench that my woodworker brother Larry crafted and placed in front of the house. We considered the text that would go on a plaque. Larry's idea is to get to the point.

> Back in Happy Days when families roamed this street, we resided here. A '57 Chevy in the driveway. Kids playing ball, riding bikes, going to music lessons. The Euclid of old, a different place, a different time.

When I arrived back home for our Christmas Day gathering, the bench was occupied. There sat Franken, the newest addition to the neighborhood. While getting acquainted, I had a thing or two to share about our family home, our refuge for five generations. As it turned out, Franken had some words to share with me.

Judy talks to Franken

Judy and Franken

Franken, I love seeing you here, waving to the many passersby who are walking, biking, and driving on this busy street, often on their way to classes, work, ballgames, and activities at the nearby campus. Some fitness enthusiasts are passing by the house—and you—before crossing the street to climb the 176 steep steps that lead to a vista of the neighborhood and the city with its landmarks and parks, its drumlins and lakes.

When my Grandpa (also known as Poppy or Pa) bought this two-family home in the spring of 1951, he had lots of company. There was Grandma, who passed away before the year was over, two daughters—my mother Gertrude and my Aunt Jeanette, my dad Sam, and seven kids. In time, another baby added to the tumult of a lively family home.

We lived upstairs, and our Pa and the others lived downstairs. It made no difference whether you lived up or down, since doors were rarely closed and never locked. Pa, a very handy man, always seemed to be painting, wallpapering, chipping plaster, making a little hole into a big one in one room or another. If there wasn't enough to do upstairs or downstairs, he was outdoors, pouring concrete to repair the sidewalk.

There was a steady flow up and down the back stairs to see what was cooking. The scent of Aunt Jeanette's famous chocolate cake, marbled with red and green and yellow, wafted up the stairs and beckoned us downward. With my most precious and talented mother often at her piano, the chords and melodies welcomed the downstairs cousins to trek up the stairs and sing along. In the warmer months, with doors and windows open, the neighbors, too, had the pleasure of hearing music, music, music.

When my dad bought a spanking new Chevy wagon in 1957, Mom insisted on having three rows of seats. After all, Dad had many kids to transport to parks, beaches, bakeries, diners, grocery stores, the movies, music lessons, friends' homes, you name it. Always chomping on a juicy cigar and whistling a tune, he was a devoted husband and father and a cherished Uncle Sam.

Franken, there is so much to tell you about the many people who basked in the closeness, warmth, and love that permeated this family and this home. But I see that you have something to say. I'm all ears.

Franken's turn

Yes, Judy. I like to listen and learn, but I also like to talk.

Let's start with my name. There once was a Victor Frankenstein who, in a science experiment, created a not-so-lovable creature who had no name, though many called him Frankenstein, after his creator. On the other hand, I do have a name. Just so you know—I am Franken, a very lovable, very kind presence. From my comfortable bench here, I greet and welcome the visitors to this house and all passersby.

Most people around here smile when they see me. They pause. They laugh. They sometimes sit beside me and take a selfie. Then, they strike a conversation with your brother—my creator—who might be dressing me up with a new hat or handing me a beer or a billiard cue or a rake.

Frankly, this Franken is having a blast watching the goings-on with my big, open eyes and listening to a cacophony of neighborhood sounds with my big, open ears. I love getting to know this neighborhood, including you and those who came before.

The cypress bench in front of this house is a beauty. It is the perfect place for you, for me, and for others to have a seat and simply lighten up in this new year and for many years to come.

Franken cheers on his favorite team, "Go SU!"

Update

Sadly, Franken met his demise, and one morning he was simply gone. A phone caller indicated he now rested at the bottom of a nearby lake. Those who became accustomed to visiting with this Franken really miss him.

'Tis the Season...

Blog posting December 21, 2017

'Tis the season of lights. Whether a flame that miraculously flickers long past the expected time, an antidote that casts out darkness, or a beacon that guides, lights glow—just like Rudolph's shiny nose. When our own light shines, we, too, sparkle. We radiate. We wear an aura that makes our world a bit brighter.

During this season, let your light shine by dwelling in a happy place. Bask in memories of moments that put a smile on your face, pep in your step, and warmth in your heart.

I will do the same, right here, right now.

Recipient

One morning, I stopped, as I often do, for breakfast. I read a little, collect my thoughts, and scribble a few to-do notes. I eat, I drink, I pay, and I leave. On this day, the check for my breakfast did not arrive. When I asked the waitress for it, she said, "You're all set." While placing a tip on the table, she added, "You're all set with that, too." A patron at the restaurant gave the waitress money to pay for someone's breakfast. "I chose you," the waitress said. That was one delicious start to my day.

On another morning, at a different venue, I purchased coffee to go and later discovered a surprise treat in the bag, something yummy to enjoy with my coffee. I stopped in the next day to say thank-you and pay for this item when I learned that this treat was a freebie. Why? "Because I like your face." How sweet is that.

"Thank you for coming here today." That's the greeting I regularly heard at a client site whenever I arrived to do some work. Before I settled in to tackle a writing project, I was in a happy mood. How nice to hear words of appreciation said with sincerity.

Arriving home one winter day, my car just wouldn't make it up my snowy, icy driveway. The more I tried, the more the wheels spun. I was plain stuck. A young man walking home from school stopped and offered, "I can push." And push he did until my car was out of the rut and safely parked in the garage. Then he insisted I hand him a shovel. "I really want to clear your driveway. It will be good for me." What a guy.

I am aglow remembering these thoughtful acts of kindness that I received.

Witness

I recently watched a friend wrap gifts she purchased for each member of a family. She does not know this family. She only knows that during this holiday season, a family is in need.

When told that storm victims from warmer climates were preparing for a cold winter in our community, I watched others in my circle rally with coats or cash to buy them.

Not too long ago, I witnessed a flurry of phone calls to alert others to a situation that required their immediate help. The timely generosity of many made someone's difficulty bearable.

On visits to a familiar neighborhood, I noticed that one individual installed a large garbage can in an area where there are many passersby. Another individual I know regularly empties it so that the contents do not overflow.

Remembering these touching moments puts me in a happy place.

Your turn

How about you? What memories of kindnesses received or witnessed warm your heart and set you aglow like our friend Rudolph?

A Team to Pull Your Sleigh

Blog posting December 20, 2014

You have a book that's waiting...for you. It's in your head. It's in your heart. It's in your bones. You can feel it wanting to take shape and become alive.

Purchase a journal, your future book. Now, pick it up. Maybe you're apprehensive, wondering how you are going to fill these empty pages, how you are going to make a book that, next year, will have a place at the table of a book sale, a place in which others can peruse your book, purchase it, read it, benefit from it, and enjoy it. Now, relax a bit. Take a deep breath, because, like Santa, who is arriving very soon, you have a team that helps you carry the load. You have your very own Rudolph, your own Dasher, Dancer, Donder, and Blitzen.

> You have Writer, Designer, and
>
> Researcher, Reviewer, and
>
> Editor, Publisher, and
>
> Printer, Bookseller, and
>
> As you may recall, you have
>
> The most famous one of all
>
> Your very own Rudolph, your Muse,
>
> With a passion so bright,
>
> Who guides your book to light.

In your journal, your future book, write "Dedication" at the top of one page; on another page, write

"Acknowledgments." Consider now the team pulling your sleigh, the team making your book real. Add their names to your book. Of course, this will change over time, but you don't need to wait for your book to be complete to think about those you will thank, the contributors who will appear in your "Dedication" and "Acknowledgments."

Let's start with your muse. Who or what is inspiring you to write this book? Add the muse to the "Dedication." When it comes to creating content for your book, who will do the research? Some of the content may come from your own life experiences; some may come from what others have written. Determine the source of your content. Consider the raw material needed to write your book.

Are you the writer? Who is helping you in this role, which also involves organizing your content into a readable, usable, interesting whole?

The visual appeal of your book is what attracts readers. If you have a traditional publisher for your book, discuss the design. Learn how much involvement you will have with the book size, the layout, the font, the artwork both in the interior and on the covers. If you are self-publishing your book, be sure to include a graphic designer on your team.

Reviewers include those who keep you out of trouble. They give you feedback and advice. Content reviewers check for accuracy. Legal reviewers check that you are not infringing on others' intellectual property.

Among the reviewers are editors who check that the organization, the book's architecture, is the best way to tell your story. Editors also check that you are using the language skillfully. Yes, that means correct grammar, capitalization, punctuation, word choice, spelling, and more. Your readers deserve, and are paying for, attention to every detail.

Who is the publisher of your book? What name, logo, and address will go in the front matter of your book? To have a traditional publisher or to self-publish? That is the question.

A traditional publisher takes care of printing your book. As a self-publisher, the option I selected was an on-demand printer. There are many, and you will want to compare their services. The one I use has features I like, such as the ability to replace cover and interior files any time I uncover a glitch, 24-7 phone support, online tracking of sales, and deposit of royalties every month (a nice, passive source of income).

Now, who sells your books? My books are available at online retailers, such as Amazon.com. Once purchased, the interaction between the buyer and printer is transparent to me. Of course, I can purchase books at a discounted rate from the printer and sell them wherever and to whomever I like.

Where do you find a Dasher, a Dancer, a Donder, a Blitzen, a Rudolph to pull your sleigh, to lighten your load? Do some research. You'll discover many resources, both online and in print. Ask other authors for advice. And, above all, hold the reins on the services you purchase. Make a book that makes sense, both for your wallet and for you.

Wellness and Happiness— As Easy as ABC

Blog posting December 5, 2012

Every month can be a busy month. Yet December with holidays, festivities, and year-end wrap-ups can make us feel especially frenzied. What to do? Apply what you already know about good health and happiness. Find ways to keep your reservoir full. Wellness and happiness can be as easy as A, B, and C.

A. Know when you are in a downward spiral. You might be working less efficiently and productively than usual. Perhaps you are experiencing boredom or displaying negativity at those with whom you work and live. If you do not feel motivated and challenged, there might be too much stress or insufficient positive stress. Take time to figure out what you need to remove from—or add to—your daily routine.

B. If too much to do seems to be converging on you, lighten up. De-clutter. Put projects away. Take them out only when you are working on them. And if you do not need that rarely used tool, that outdated furniture, or that stack of old magazines, books, and games, get rid of it. If others can use your discards, then sell them or donate them. If not, recycle them or toss them.

C. Get physical. Get mental. See what classes are available to keep your body and mind in motion. Your health insurer, community center, school district, supermarket, sporting goods store, or library may be offering just the right program for you. Whether it's aerobics, dance, or zumba; healthy cooking, weight reduction, or nutrition; first aid, anger management, or a book club—find a new activity and find it now.

As for me, I am going to

A. Laugh each day.

B. Say adieu to oversized clothes.

C. Stretch my brain by making *Career Success in 12 Easy Steps: A Journal* the first book in a trilogy. Yes, that means two more books are waiting to be authored.

How about you? What are your happiness and wellness plans? They can be as easy as ABC.

Update

After *Career Success in 12 Easy Steps: A Journal*, I wrote two more books. These three books compose a trilogy—my Living Well series. *A Step, a Stroll, a Blog, a Book: Collecting My Thoughts* makes book number four.

Writing

Wood Works Wonders

Blog posting March 13, 2014

My writing desk is a work in progress.

While you are looking at this photo of a work in progress, I am marveling over the real deal—the varnished, cherry writing desk, now with knobs on the two drawers and a panel that goes over the drawer on the left to provide additional surface.

From the unfinished writing desk that my brother Larry and my cousin Marty are modeling in the photo, you can likely tell that this is homemade. Larry, our family's very own woodworker and furniture maker, asked me what I'd like at the start of this very tough upstate New York winter. Answering Larry's question was easy. I wanted a writer's desk.

I found a few images, requested some modifications (such as book ends), provided the desired dimensions, and left everything else in Larry's adept hands. And those hands, along with those of our brother Richard, delivered the finished desk this week to a corner of an upstairs room in what will be my writer's nook.

Unlike my first-floor home office, furnished with all the electronic gizmos needed to run a technical writing business and open to visitors, my nook will be my space, with journals and notebooks (paper, not electronic), stationery, pencils, and books. I will add some meaningful items—the two lovely watercolors that Paula, an artist and my late mother's home aide, sent me with her treasured note, "I miss her very much!...She was a great conversationalist and tremendously gifted piano player. I respected her very much." In my sacred space, I will read and find comfort.

For now, I have moved a chair from downstairs to upstairs and am getting ready to sit and read and think and wonder and write. I'm not sure if it is the varnish or the cherry or both, but the smell alone refreshes. I am getting ready to work wonders.

Where is that special nook, retreat, or sanctuary that inspires *you*?

Update

No longer a work in progress, my writer's desk is the perfect spot to write a note on this wintry day.

Audiences Might Like to Know...

Blog posting September 1, 2017

I am a published author. In 2011, I published my first book, *Career Success in 12 Easy Steps: A Journal.* In 2014, I published my second book, *A Bisl of This, A Bisl of That: Eating Our Way.* In 2017, I published my third book, *Living Well in Froggy's World of Plenty: Sweet Talk to Read.* At this rate, book four should be ready in 2020. Yikes. It's almost time to consider a topic.

In the meantime, I'm going to write a talk that I can deliver to audiences, sharing my experiences authoring, publishing, and promoting my books. What will I say?

That depends on what audiences want to know. For now, I'll put my imagination to work and think about one member of my audience—you.

Living Well in Froggy's World of Plenty

You might like to know that before I started writing about Froggy and his critter friends, I could feel a book percolating. Then on Leap Year day, February 29, 2016, the bubbles surfaced. Froggy has a wart that one day is gone, gone, gone. He isn't sure how this happened. Froggy, Flutter By, Orchid, Sweetie B, Bobalong Bird, and their other critter friends would help me to explore and discover healing and wellness.

You might like to know that while writing about Froggy, I was ensconced in a happy place. I sat at the beautiful cherry writer's desk that my woodworker brother built especially for me. Using a new laptop computer, I wrote in brief stints of maybe an hour or so before starting my workday. From the window, I looked at the changing seasons and let the stories—30 or so slices of life—write themselves.

You might like to know that while writing about Froggy, it occurred to me that, if Mom were still alive, she would be 100 on May 28, 2017. That gave me a goal. Books would be in hand to distribute to family and friends who would gather on that day. I am happy to say, "Mission accomplished."

A Bisl of This, A Bisl of That

You might like to know about the origins for this book—a combination cookbook, inspiration, and memoir. I called my cousin to wish her well on upcoming surgery. The worrying tone changed when I asked for one of Grandma's famous recipes. "Let's start a cookbook," she suggested. "You send an email to all the cousins, with a copy to me, requesting favorite recipes," I responded. And so it began.

You might like to know that a few recipes trickled in. Then a few more arrived. I forwarded all arriving emails so that the cousins and others could see how this project was taking shape. More recipes arrived as well as requests to include Larry's potato latkes (pancakes), Aunt Jeanette's stuffed cabbage, Mom's chocolate sponge cake, Grandma's special mile-high lemon meringue pie. Stories accompanied the recipes and the requests—heartwarming remembrances of cooks and kitchens that continue to nourish and sustain.

You might like to know the requests have not stopped. "Where is the recipe for chicken soup?" "What, no challah (braided bread)?" "No half-moon cookies?" At book-signing events, I'm often asked to find a treasured recipe. "My Grandmother came from...and made the most delicious..." "My brother would be so happy if you could find our Great Aunt Sarah's recipe for..." I do my best to find the sought-after recipe.

Career Success in 12 Easy Steps

You might like to know that I was spending too many hours in front of a computer, writing manuals for clients and managing a technical writing business. Working from a home-based office, I missed being with people. I remembered my teaching days and the exchanges that take place in classrooms and group settings. I wanted to get out more to talk and listen and created a plan to transition from here to there. Thus, a book was born.

You might like to know that I submitted my book proposal to three traditional publishers. A year later, with three rejections in hand, a chance encounter with a colleague familiar with my technical writing business said, "You don't need a publisher. Just write your book and publish it." And so I did.

You might like to know that one day I was at a community event, visiting the various displays. One table that caught my eye was about high school competitions for building robots. I had been wondering if *Career Success in 12 Easy Steps* might be appropriate for high schoolers, showed the robotics coach the proof copy I had with me, and asked for his opinion. He perused the book. We talked. Then he said, "I have a book budget and will buy a book for each member of my teams." True to his word, he did just that. Selling 200 or so books in one fell swoop certainly caught my attention and helped my wallet.

Your turn

Now you know some of the back story of my three books. What more do you think audiences would like to know about authors and their books?

Update

In 2017, I wrote that book four should be ready in 2020. That did not happen. What did happen, though, is the creation of one eBook in 2019, another eBook in 2020, an eLearning companion in 2021, and this book (eBook and print versions) to welcome in 2022.

Pour Patterns, Thoughts, Connections, and Ideas onto Paper

Blog posting May 9, 2012

In a recent phone interview, the conversation centered around journaling—specifically, what I call guided journaling. This is the technique used in *Career Success in 12 Easy Steps: A Journal* to move readers, journalers, and seekers of career success from steps 1 and 2, "Wake up to Your Dreams" and "Build on Your Successes," all the way to steps 11 and 12, "Bestow Unto Others" and "And Also Receive." This approach can work for all kinds of success—business, professional, personal, retirement, and more.

Like a friend or confidante, guided journaling takes the reader by the hand. Your guide tells stories that inspire you, provides quotes that resonate, asks question that probe, and, throughout, affirms you as a capable person. Each page in a guided journal invites a response, opening your mind and heart to possibilities.

Guided journaling offers a way to reflect, gain clarity, discover your right livelihood, create a plan, and take actions. Remembering and owning past successes builds confidence, motivation, and energy, fueling new dreams that propel you forward.

There is power to pouring tired patterns, errant thoughts, disjointed connections, and fresh ideas onto paper. Here the life of the mind becomes a separate entity with which to interact.

If you prefer starting with a blank page, keep a notebook with you and write, write, write. If you want a journal that guides you along, peruse the bookstore for that perfect guided journaling tool. Consider sharing your journaling journey with a friend, coach, teacher, parent, spouse, or group. As life's possibilities unfold for you, let us hear from you.

It Takes an Acrobat to Organize Content

Blog posting July 30, 2013

If you are a communicator of technical, marketing, business, or information, at least one of your projects today likely involves organizing content. You might be wondering, "What should I consider when deciding on an effective organizational pattern to use? What's a good way to structure topics into a logical, orderly flow? How can I combine multiple topics into fewer topics? What are some of my options for organizing content?"

In a webinar I presented to the Society for Technical Communication, "Patterns for Organizing Content — Many More than A to Z," participants had activities to work through independently. Let's look at one of those activities together.

Organize content deliverables for your employer

Your department is developing a promotional piece, *Our Content Deliverables*, for your employer. How would you organize the following content deliverables?

> case studies, catalogs, courseware, diagnostics and troubleshooting, instructions, marketing collateral, online help, operations and maintenance, parts lists, proposals, reports, scripts, service manuals, software instructions, specifications and requirements, speeches,

standard operating procedures, strategic plans, style guides, theory of operations, training material, user guides, and website content

You might agree that this alphabetical listing is one option for organizing a list, but it is not particularly effective. There is no logical flow to assist the reader. Consider how your employer is accustomed to thinking about content. Perhaps your employer organizes work according to lifecycles, in which a product progresses through various phases. To be in step with your employer, try organizing your promotional piece according to where each content deliverable belongs in the product lifecycle. For example:

- Developing and testing the product might include reports, specifications and requirements, standard operating procedures, strategic plans, and style guides.

- Marketing and selling the product might include case studies, catalogs, marketing collateral, parts lists, proposals, speeches, and website content.

- Servicing the product might include diagnostics and troubleshooting, operations and maintenance, service manuals, and a theory of operations.

- Training the end user of the product might include courseware, instructions, online help, scripts, software instructions, training material, and user guides.

Of course, the placement of the content deliverables is somewhat arbitrary. Different writers have different ideas, but grouping the content deliverables into categories that have a common heading (in this case the phase in the product lifecycle) helps the reader to see relationships among various content deliverables, similarities with content deliverables in the same phase of the lifecycle, and differences from deliverables listed in another phase of the lifecycle. Reading a promotional piece that organizes your content deliverables by their placement in the product lifecycle may just prompt your employer to use your services when developing and testing a product, marketing and selling, servicing it, and training end users. It can open opportunities for you—just what you hoped your promotional piece would accomplish.

Organize content deliverables for your client

Now, let's assume your promotional piece that describes your many content deliverables is intended for your client who organizes his business according to internal and external offerings. You might organize your list the same way as your client. For example:

- Internal content deliverables—those that never leave the company—might include diagnostics and troubleshooting, service manuals, specifications and requirements, standard operating procedures, strategic plans, and style guides.

- External content deliverables—those that the world outside the company sees—might include case studies, catalogs, courseware, instructions, marketing collateral, online help, operations and maintenance, parts lists, proposals, reports, scripts, software instructions, speeches, theory of operations, training material, user guides, and website content.

Again, you're thinking like your client and organizing your promotional piece in a way that is familiar, comfortable, and easy to digest.

There's more to do

Now, revisit the four bulleted items for the employer and the two bulleted items for the client. Currently the content deliverables within each item are organized alphabetically. You can do better than that. Give it a try and use an organizational pattern that you consider effective. Being agile, nimble, and quick means being open to ways of organizing content that make sense to you and resonate with your readers. What organizing patterns do you like to use? Do you have favorites? We'd love to hear about them.

Inspire Thyself

Blog posting September 30, 2013

You, too, can inspire thyself.

In-spire. Yes, breathe in. Take in some fresh air. Become refreshed. Become renewed. Look, listen, touch, smell, and taste from the many creations in art, crafts, literature, movies, music, and nature that surround you. Many of these sources of inspiration are others' creations. Yet, some sources may come from you—at an earlier time, perhaps in a different place. Look back at your work, and let it move you to something better, something great, maybe even something profound.

In the two plus years that *Career Success in 12 Easy Steps: A Journal* has been available, I have written blogs and presentation material for seminars and webinars—all intended to inspire and motivate others—and myself—to move their life in a positive direction.

And now is a time to pause, to reflect on my own words.

"See yourself as a whole person, a human being who is capable, qualified, and well-equipped to do the task. ... Do not become an obstacle to your success. See yourself as you could yet become. See your competencies, strengths, achievements, and potential. Find opportunities—flawed and imperfect as you are—to grow and thrive." Source: "Give Away that Which You Hope to Receive"

"Signs of innate talents and aptitudes become apparent, evolve, and are always there. Many options exist for ways to use these talents and aptitudes. We learn what we need to know to succeed at our work. From novice to competent worker to specialist to expert, we evolve. Sparks emerge. Energy ignites. Motivation is present. Inspiration appears. Something happens unexpectedly. We like what we are doing. We are good at it. Others notice. We notice." Source: Shenouda journaling notes

"Earlier dreams have crystallized. We have already succeeded in fulfilling some of our dreams—at least partially. Dreams change and evolve. Our new dream may not be new at all. It may simply be a variation on a theme. We can own the dream—and then take action." Source: Shenouda journaling notes

"Guided journaling offers a way to reflect, gain clarity, discover your right livelihood, create a plan, and take actions. Remembering and owning past successes builds confidence, motivation, and energy, fueling new dreams that propel you forward." Source: "Pour Patterns, Thoughts, Connections, and Ideas onto Paper"

Career Success in 12 Easy Steps: A Journal has served me well. It has become a repository, a wellspring for ideas to explore in writing and in talking. And I have continued to do both. Presentations developed and delivered include "Accentuate the Positive," "Wake Up to Your Dreams," "Own Your Competencies,"

"Communicate Your Value," "Keep Your Reservoir Full," and "Create a Successful Work and Life."

As part of a troupe of speakers committed to communicating new ideas, improving communities for good, and simply being awesome, more opportunities to write and talk, to grow and thrive are clearly in view.

So how about you? Looking back, what have you created that inspires you today? I would love to know.

The eLearning Companion to Career Success in 12 Easy Steps: A Journal

Blog posting September 30, 2021

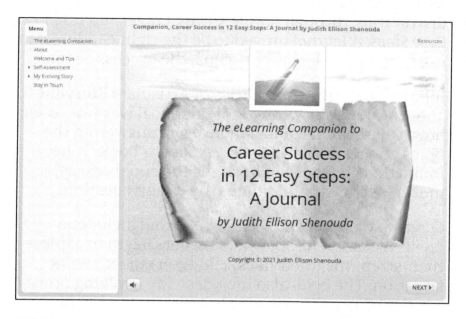

With a pandemic looming and lingering, a long period of sheltering in place presented an opportunity to move back-burner projects to the forefront. With a pause in client work, both this business owner and employees could focus on some fun stuff. Long-time employee Julia expressed an interest in learning Articulate Storyline 360 to create eLearning content. The question was, "What existing content could we use?"

For 35 years, Shenouda Associates Inc. has created technical and business publications for clients, from guides that show users how a product works to manuals that service engineers use when installing equipment, replacing parts, doing adjustments, and more. Over the past 10 years, I have authored and published my own books, both in print and eBook formats. With the help of my extraordinary employees, these books have been inside jobs, from writing and editing, to designing and publishing, to distributing through online stores. *Career Success in 12 Easy Steps: A Journal* proved to be the right candidate to use for eLearning content. Thus, the process began.

Julia explored the capabilities of Articulate Storyline 360. Early on, she wrote, "My first goal was just to see how well the tool could handle users answering the types of questions in the *Career Success* book." She found that the tool could handle the book's essay, multiple-choice, and fill-in-the-blank questions.

Career Success in 12 Easy Steps: A Journal includes a "Self-Assessment" in which readers begin to explore their strengths, their likes, and their current work situation. The book also includes "My Evolving Story," a series of 12 stories (each aligned with one of the 12 steps to career success) in which readers fill in the blanks to write their own story for moving forward at work or in other life endeavors. The "Self-Assessment" and "My Evolving Story" are the backbone of the eLearning companion.

Julia continued to learn the tool and communicate her progress. Throughout the development process, I set the direction, reviewed drafts, and offered feedback.

With the eLearning ready to share, the focus now is finding organizations and groups that can benefit from using it as a standalone tool, a companion to the book, or in preparation for an instructor-led workshop.

I applaud Julia's desire to learn Articulate Storyline 360 and consider the resulting eLearning product impressive and useful.

I Helped You. I Received My Reward. The Score Is Even.

Blog posting December 2, 2011

I was inspired recently when a colleague said that the best birthday present for her upcoming big day would be reading about others' good deeds. Since getting my recent book into the hands, hearts, and minds of those who could benefit continues to be a top priority, I set out to do just that, believing that doing so would be a good deed.

At various meetings and events, I have given away my book as a door prize. At times, I have given away more copies than I intended, just because I felt like it. And guess what? Recipients purchased copies—for the 20-something child seeking direction, the recently downsized friend, the local library. I have received flowers and dinner, referrals to speak at meetings, and the wonderful company of new friends.

What I learned about doing good should not surprise you. You likely know this already. When you give, somehow it comes back to you, from somewhere. My mother—ever a source of wisdom—told me that years ago, a Mr. P visited regularly to provide spiritual support. Together, they read religious texts and talked about many aspects of their life, including the challenges that Mr. P faced with his children who were struggling. In time, Mr. P and his family moved away. Some time later, when Mom received a letter from Mr. P, she learned that his children were thriving. To this day, she believes that this letter from Mr. P carried a bigger message: *I helped you. I received my reward. The score is even.* Enough said.

On your big day, dear colleague, smile, laugh, and delight in reading of the many good deeds that those in our midst do, day in and day out.

Sweeten Your Days

Blog posting September 29, 2014

Once a book is authored, published, and printed, there's the added joy of sharing the finished product. At a recent outdoor music and cultural festival, I did just that. With the goal that *A Bisl of This, A Bisl of That: Eating Our Way* reach those who could benefit, the festival was wonderful in so many ways.

A festival

Because the festival was in Syracuse, NY, my hometown, my family who live in the area gathered in a show of support. My brothers Larry and Richard delivered and set up a long table with chairs to display my books. My young grandniece Kara set out the tablecloth, arranged books and business cards, filled the candy jar, and displayed a plaque with the words, "I love you a bushel and a peck and a hug around the neck." My nephews Jacob and David and others stood watch. Our table looked very inviting.

The first person to stop by bought *A Bisl of This, A Bisl of That: Eating Our Way*. She noted that the $18 price tag was a very good sign, since 18 is the number for Chai, which is Hebrew for life. Passers-by perused the book, delighted to find recipes for food they love, contributed by, in some cases, people they knew. I discovered that foodies love to cook, bake, eat—and talk.

I was happy to meet Kara's friend Sophie. It turned out that her mom is the second cousin of one of my oldest and dearest Syracuse friends who has some recipes in the book. It was my pleasure to give Sophie's mom my book as a thank-you for her kindness to Kara.

A childhood friend Myra and her adult daughter Lisa stopped by. I had not seen them in 25 years and pointed out that Rose, who was Myra's mom and Lisa's grandmother, gave my mom (my much loved Ma) a wonderful recipe for strudel, which is included in the "Cookies and Pastries" section of my book.

When I recognized a passerby as a member of the clergy who, faithfully and compassionately, visited my dear Ma daily during her final days, I greeted him but could not speak for several long moments, viscerally feeling again those difficult days. In gratitude for his support, I gave him *A Bisl of This, A Bisl of That: Eating Our Way* where he will get to know my Ma at her best as well as the many loved ones she nourished.

My cousin Maxine greeted visitors to our table, sharing her enthusiasm for the recipes and snippets of family lore that season the book's pages. My sister Sandy stopped by just in time to hear a gentleman named Harold describe a recipe that his mother brought with her from Europe many years ago.

A recipe

At home, from her collection of treasured recipes, Sandy retrieved a recipe for plum kuchen that looked very close to the recipe Harold described. She wrote, "Mrs. M always brought it for holiday meals or a

Sunday pizza night. She was a terrific cook. I'm sure this recipe came with her from Germany." May this plum kuchen—provided here for Harold and for you— sweeten your days.

Plum kuchen

1. Sift into a bowl: 1 1/2 cups flour; 2 tsp baking powder; 1/2 tsp salt; and 1/2 cup sugar

2. Add to the bowl and cut the mixture until it is crumbly: 1/2 cup oil

3. Add to the bowl and stir until moist: 1 egg, beaten; and 1/2 cup milk

4. Spread the dough onto a greased 9 x 9 in. square pan

5. On top of the dough, add: 12 large plums, halved, pitted, and sliced; and a mixture of 1/2 cup sugar and 1/2 tsp cinnamon

6. Drizzle with: 3 tbsp melted butter

7. Bake at 350 for 40 minutes

P.S. Harold said his mother's recipe also included prunes and apples. If you like, just include those with the plums. Her topping also had walnuts, which you can easily mix with the sugar and cinnamon. Sound delicious? Give it a try, and enjoy.

Business

My Job: Taking Care of Business

Blog posting June 16, 2015

In the spring of 1985, I was working in a career services office for a university when a request came from a corporate manager for someone to write a policies and procedures manual. Though I had not worked in corporate America and had not written a manual, a colleague encouraged me to apply. With a degree in Public Communication and a major in Literacy Journalism, I had solid writing skills. I took the four-month assignment, enjoyed the work, did it well, resigned from the university, worked through an agency on a variety of technical and business writing projects, and, a year later, launched my own business.

Part of what I love about running Shenouda Associates Inc. is the ability to schedule my own time. By now, I know what needs to be done to keep the business humming along. My calendar is filled with key dates, so that at the start of any given week, I can set priorities. No longer is every day or every hour booked, which means I have the luxury of doing some of my own creative work, including self-publishing my own books.

Overall, my job includes activities in the administrative, human resources (HR), and marketing areas and, of course, many day-to-day activities revolve around the craft of researching, writing, editing, and publishing.

Administrative activities include time spent tracking progress on projects, billing clients, preparing a payroll, and assuring that the business is taking in more than it is spending. In a nutshell, this is time invested in taking care of business—essential to any business's success.

At Shenouda Associates Inc., I am the **HR** department. As someone who enjoys spending time with people and getting to know them, I regularly go to meetings and events of professional organizations such as the Society for Technical Communication (STC) and often meet others who are candidates for projects. Over time, I have developed a cadre of human resources, with a variety of skills, who can work on technical communication and related projects.

Marketing is an ongoing pursuit. By now, I have all kinds of collaterals—a printed presentation folder, business card, brochure; as well as a website, blog, and online presence in social networking sites—that convey our capabilities. When potential or current clients want to know how we can meet specific communication needs, I write project proposals and statements of work. Once the project is in hand, these tools evolve into tracking tools, assuring that the business delivers what was promised.

Some portion of each week and often each day is spent on the **craft** of a technical and business communicator. Currently, I am analyzing a series of websites in a vertical market and documenting the elements on each page, writing a service manual for a client's new product, and organizing and editing the contents of a book that a client will self-publish. With others in my business involved in writing, editing, and publishing a variety of print and electronic deliverables for clients,

I am often another pair of eyes or hands, doing whatever is needed to hand off a quality deliverable.

My job is more than doing administrative, HR, marketing, and craft-related activities. It is about creating value by fulfilling our promise: *Shenouda eases communication*, making the world work just a little bit better—manual by manual, publication by publication, book by book.

Conference Notes

Blog posting November 1, 2012

Are you thinking of attending a professional conference? Are you weighing the cons with the pros? Sure, this will cost you money—likely out of your own pocket—and time. While you're away, that looming project deadline will not disappear. Neither will that family event. Yet, you'd like a change of scenery. You could benefit from a renewed sense of purpose. You know it's time to recharge. You decide to go.

A while ago, I committed to doing a presentation at an out-of-town conference of technical communicators and made my travel arrangements. Early last week, I got my act together, finalizing my presentation, taking care of responsibilities on the business and home front, and preparing myself for a few days away.

Upon Friday's arrival in Knoxville, Tennessee, I was taking in new sights—the converging rivers, rolling green hills, and falling, red, autumn leaves—and new sounds, including the respectful "Miss Judy" or "Ma'm" of the student volunteers who transported me between the conference and the hotel. Throughout my stay, I enjoyed Southern warmth and hospitality and an abundance of food, food, food with desserts, desserts, desserts—delicious indulgences.

Besides the ambiance, the sessions I attended proved to be valuable, relevant, and inspirational. I especially enjoyed Dr. Mark Littmann's approach to "Science Writing That Thrills the Public." Participants critiqued several examples of science writing, ranging from the dry to the poetic. And he shared how we, too, can write with accuracy and respect for our readers, involving them as witnesses to an unfolding story. Dr. Russel Hirst shared how to "Write as You Would Be Written to." One of the key take-aways for me is that like so much else in our world, moderation rules. Writing has a sweet place in which there are enough words—not more, not fewer—to convey your message and make your point. Fred O'Hara's talk, "So Why Don't We *Get* Global Change?," showed how to explain global warming—or any complex topic—to the public. I hope that those who attended my session, "Creating a Successful Work and Life," learned from the example of success and wellness that I provided—the transformation from Robert Rushing to Robert Renewed.

I returned home with new titles to share with my book club, new techniques to apply to my own writing, and a better understanding of the effect of the sun, the rotation of the earth, and the warming oceans on climate. Fortunately, my connecting flight left LaGuardia just hours before raging, superstorming Sandy flooded the area and wrought so much destruction and heartache. There is much to ponder from a few days away at a conference.

Have you benefited from time away? Care to share your conference notes?

Your Goods Have Value

Blog posting September 13, 2012

My book, *Career Success in 12 Easy Steps: A Journal*, offers a step-by-step approach to creating a successful life at work, in a career, and beyond. Laying out the steps to achieving goals makes the journey manageable. A topic that comes up frequently for me—and likely for you—is identifying and conveying the value that our work, our products, our services, our offerings provide. In business terms, that translates to a *value proposition*—the savings in time and cost, the improvements that result, the ability of our client to succeed, and more. A value proposition lets our clients and others know that we understand them and that we have *goods*—in every sense of the word—that are different from and better than those of others.

This takes me to my 12-step process—"Step 3: Own Your Competencies." After all, our competencies are integral to the value we provide clients, employers, employees, colleagues, and just about anyone with whom we interact. Our competencies include our knowledge, abilities, talents, skills, and gifts that add up to our strengths. They become the differentiators that make each of us and our offerings unique.

In Step 3, you meet Paul Player, a very competent poker player who is learning that his ability to think positively, make strategic and tactical decisions, see below the surface, and work and play well with others—learned from playing poker—are strengths that add value to his goods. If Paul were to teach a course, it would be about poker, including the decision-making abilities and people skills he has learned from the game.

What do you do well—and even better than almost anyone else you know? Let us suppose that others have noticed this strength and have asked you to teach a course. What would you teach? What assignments would you include? What materials would you use? What will students learn? What skills will enable them to succeed in the course? If you were asked to write a book, broadcast a YouTube video, or create a game to support your course, what would you include? What would you name it? Why?

Think about your many strengths and capabilities and the value they can provide. Think about who can benefit from what you offer. Think about how you can benefit, as well.

As for Paul Player, he will continue to excel at his poker game and win some cash every now and then. His love of the game, his skill, and his intrigue with the tactics and strategies for winning have inspired him to enter the gaming industry.

To convey his capabilities and influence the decision-makers who can hire him, he has crafted this value proposition for a company that creates online games, including poker:

> I am an expert poker player who dreams of creating new games that others and I will love to play. My passion for the game and desire to make it the passion of the many visitors to your website bode well for your continued success as

the number one product developer in the online gaming industry. I offer you my skills, my energies, and my talents as a poker player in the role of a product specialist for your company.

Now, based on your many competencies, go ahead and craft your value proposition. We would love to see you succeed in sharing your goods with those who can benefit.

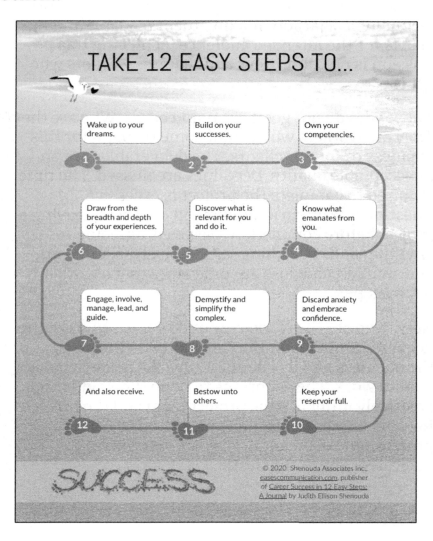

TAKE 12 EASY STEPS TO...

1. Wake up to your dreams.
2. Build on your successes.
3. Own your competencies.
4. Know what emanates from you.
5. Discover what is relevant for you and do it.
6. Draw from the breadth and depth of your experiences.
7. Engage, involve, manage, lead, and guide.
8. Demystify and simplify the complex.
9. Discard anxiety and embrace confidence.
10. Keep your reservoir full.
11. Bestow unto others.
12. And also receive.

SUCCESS

© 2020 Shenouda Associates Inc., easescommunication.com, publisher of Career Success in 12 Easy Steps: A Journal by Judith Ellison Shenouda

I Am Unique and So Are You.
We Are Keepers.

Blog posting March 5, 2012

This business succeeds if workers are appropriately aligned with the business's mission, which is developing publications that simplify the tangle of technological jargon, making them readable and usable for the intended audience. Achieving this mission is no short order and requires workers who get it.

Those who do not get it are **not keepers**. Who are they? They are workers who do not come through for this business or for our clients. The deliverables are an unacceptable quality. Deadlines are missed. The time required to complete the project is excessive. Questionable integrity, talking ill of others, leaving a project before completion, passively agreeing to anything and everything, aggressively lashing out, and similar behaviors are indicators that a worker is not a keeper.

Now, who are the workers that do get it? Who are the **keepers**? Simply put, they are suited to the mission of the business and its clients. They take pride in doing quality work. They continue to hone their skills and positively influence the project team and the project. Keepers possess a strong work ethic and have a professional demeanor. They are committed, dedicated, and enthusiastic.

This employer seeks workers with the right competencies, the right attitude, the right demeanor, and the right alignment—a combination that produces the right results.

Update

The 2020 redo of our website describes keepers this way:

You benefit from our ability to recognize the keepers

Keepers are in-demand workers who

- Take pride in quality work

- Hone their skills and capabilities

- Demonstrate a strong work ethic

- Display a professional demeanor

- Show commitment, dedication, and enthusiasm

- Work and play well with others

- Solve, rather than create, problems

- Rise to the occasion without excuses, without fanfare

How Does Your Garden Grow?

Blog posting December 16, 2019

Writing is like growing a garden. As we nurture the seedlings of ideas, the results we deliver are the product of a careful, methodical writing process that starts with understanding our readers' needs and planning how to meet them.

At the start, we take a close look at the environment. We analyze the existing materials and start to picture the finished product. As the scope of work comes into focus, we map out how to move from the existing materials to the finished product. We consider how best to organize and format the deliverables. We assemble tools and break ground by creating a framework with outlines and templates. We sink our hands into the dirt, gather input from subject matter experts, and do our homework to understand the subject matter.

We place content into the right location and shape it into paragraphs, lists, tables, and other text elements. By leaving out whatever is not needed, we streamline ideas, showcasing the most important content and nurturing it to maturity.

We make sure that our creation matches our plans and feels like a balanced, unified whole. We check that the work is accurate and complete, minimizing distraction from jarring details.

As we walk through our garden, we confirm that it is easy to navigate. At harvest time, we publish our work, providing readers a bounty of new food for thought. Mature, published documents continue to grow and change with the seasons. We review and revise. We weed out what is no longer needed. We provide ongoing maintenance.

With the proper care, we allow our garden to grow.

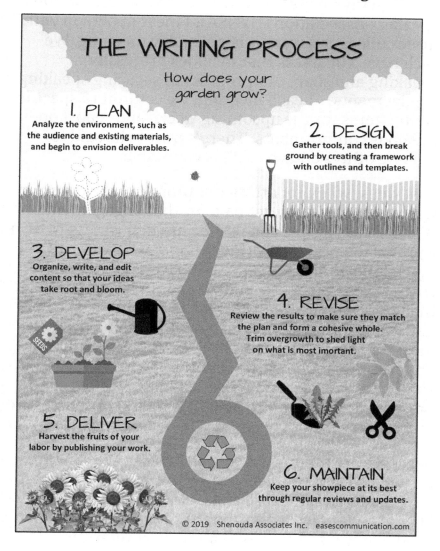

Do for Others, and Have Others Do for You

Blog posting April 8, 2012

Through my involvement with the New York National Speakers Association (NYNSA), I meet in person with three colleagues every other Monday morning. We each have a business that includes professional speaking and share our progress in securing speaking engagements. At each meeting, we commit to specific action items for the upcoming weeks and report on previous commitments. There's a lot to be said for making others and yourself accountable.

Last week, when reporting our progress, the question was posed, "Did you get paid for that engagement?" Of course, as professionals who are in business to turn a profit, the preferred answer is, "Yes." Yet we all agreed that doing some pro bono work is part of the cost of doing business, and we can find ways to make that work worthwhile. We may, for example, speak at national conference sessions or at local business meetings in which we might or might not receive an honorarium. When we do for others—in our case, sharing our expertise as professional speakers or presenters—we want to benefit. Dollars, of course, are one way.

Yet there are other ways we can benefit. We can be introduced to an audience of potential clients. We can be considered for future engagements that have budgets. We can use the opportunity to introduce our products and services. We can request referrals.

And public relations both before and after the event can widen our exposure to new audiences.

In preparation for an upcoming speaking engagement with the Rochester Professional Consultants Network (RPCN), the program coordinator created and posted a video featuring my co-presenter and me. This promotional tool has opened my mind to the many forms of payment that are available.

The next time you do pro bono work, request payment that is meaningful to you. And when you ask others to do pro bono work for you or your organization, find ways to repay them for their generosity. We need to remember that giving and receiving are two sides of the same coin.

Hurray for You

Blog posting February 11, 2012

Do you know someone who, in your eyes, is successful? He wins every game, has friends ever seeking his wise counsel, and is the go-to guy whenever a problem surface. She is the one who represents the school or the office, mediates among conflicting views, and always volunteers to do what's needed. Like you, there are people I consider winners. Yet, they sell themselves short. In their own eyes, they have not yet arrived. They believe they are just not quite good enough. Somehow, they do not see themselves as successful.

How can we help our esteemed friends to see themselves in a more positive light? We can point out the contributions they make—often unbeknownst to them—that matter to us. "Tom, thank you for providing backup support on my project. As a result, I was able to get away for a much needed break." "Sharon, I appreciate your effort arranging the event. I know it took time to find the perfect location, order the refreshments, send out notices, and greet attendees. With the details covered, I could focus on my presentation."

Tom can feel good about his ability and willingness to back up a colleague, knowing that he supported someone's wellness. Sharon can take pride in her attention to detail, knowing it contributed favorably to the overall event.

Now, how can we see ourselves as worthy, successful winners? We can pay attention when others thank us and take their appreciation to heart. And, when a thank you is not forthcoming, we can still relish in the many ways—small and large— that we do our part, knowing it makes a difference somewhere, somehow, to someone.

Now, what have you done today that benefits another? Let us know, and we promise to shout, "Hurray for you."

Yin and Yang—You Can Do a Balancing Act

Blog posting January 10, 2012

As a small business owner, I recognize the critical importance of balancing the needs of the business to deliver the products and services that clients purchase with the needs of workers who have all kinds of non-work demands on their time and energy. Over the years, I have learned to address this yin and yang balancing act.

I determine the human resources that are needed to complete all clients' projects on time. Knowing the starting point of a project (what we are receiving), the completion point (what we are delivering), and the due date, I calculate as best as I can—in spite of many unknowns—the number of people hours of work that are required each week.

It is equally important to establish with workers their availability. How many hours can they realistically work on average per work? Are these hours during our clients' typical working day? If not, when are they able to address questions from others—clients, colleagues, and me? Gaining clarity on workers' availability and constraints is key.

Knowing the human resources that are needed to meet clients' needs, I map out a solution that takes into account the time that workers can commit. Maybe a team approach is needed. Maybe I will be part of the mix, either as a backup resource or the project's *face* in team meetings. This takes creative juggling but has allowed my business to retain both loyal, long-standing clients and loyal, long-standing workers.

Communities

Good Communities—
Make Them Happen

Blog posting July 10, 2013

One of the joys of participating with several colleagues in a speaking troupe we call Thinking Forward involves creating thoughtful talks for our audience. Our latest theme, Transforming Your Community for Good, got me thinking.

What do communities look like?

Communities of people come in lots of different sizes and shapes. They may be specialized and similar or diverse and different in terms of age, gender, race, ethnicity, religion, cultural background, residence, level of education, economic status, type of employment, or some other demographic.

Communities likely have insiders and outsiders. They are exclusive in some way. Members may live in the same neighborhood. They may work for the same employer. Maybe they have the same professional degrees or licenses. Communities can have different structures. They can be hierarchical, where members fall somewhere between the top and the bottom. They can be flat, where all members have an equal voice. In some communities, you already belong. If you graduated from a specific college, you are in the community of alumni. In others, you have to join. For example, membership in an association of alumni likely makes you a more exclusive member of the community, with additional perks.

Though communities look different, members share a bond; there is common thread; there is a tie that unites. And all communities—as different as they are—are part of a global community of human beings who breathe the same air, walk the same earth, and touch one another, someway, somehow.

How do you know a good community when you see one?

Good communities can be anywhere and everywhere. And you know a good community when you see one. These communities seem to live by some sort of exemplary standard or model of excellence— sometimes written and objective; other times informal, unspoken, and subjective—that is evident and visible. You can experience their goodness. You know them by their fruits—there's love and laughter, friendship and respect, joy and kindness, compassion and strength, and so much more.

How do we create a good community?

We can follow the example of communities in which many people enjoy a good, extra long, healthy, meaningful life. According to findings in the *Reverse Engineering Longevity* study by Dan Buettner and a National Geographic team who studied the world's longest-lived people, there are communities that seem to have found the secret to living long and living well. In the Barbagia mountainous highlands of inner

Sardinia; Ikaria, Greece, an Aegean Island; Nicoya Peninsula, Costa Rica; the Seventh Day Adventists community near Loma Linda, California; and Okinawa, Japan; people behave in ways that add years to their life. They move naturally. Physical activity is built into the fabric of their daily routine—there's no need to work out at the gym. They have a purpose for waking up each morning and have rituals to shed stress. They stop eating when they are 80 % full, eat more plants and less meat, and drink wine—in moderation, daily, and with friends. Faith, family, and social networks that support healthy behaviors are part and parcel of everyday life.

Reading about the guiding principles for designing an urban landscape provides yet other clues for creating good communities. The designers' plan for creating a good city included enhancing the pedestrian experience; constructing gateways to connect districts, neighborhoods, and sites; greening the downtown area; developing the river; and creating mixed-use neighborhoods. One can only imagine the wonderful possibilities for community members to live a good life in an urban setting that is both functional and beautiful.

Your turn

Think of the many organizations in your world. Think of them as communities of individuals with shared interests, shared values, shared resources, shared space. What do the good communities in your world look like? What makes them good? What can make them even better? I'd love to hear from you.

Afformations—Forms that Say Yes

Blog posting December 18, 2011

Creating tools has been a part of my makeup for as long as I can remember. I'm not talking about hardware tools, but I am talking about job aids that guide us through a process. As a student, I converted long passages of text into outlines, charts, and other visual aids that stripped away the excess, leaving the headings, key points, and relationships. That was really all that was necessary to help me recall the whole story. As a teacher, I developed similar tools to help organize content for my students. As owner of a technical communication business, I developed tools for talking with clients to scope out jobs; identifying the qualifications that workers needed in order to complete jobs; working through the process of researching, designing, and delivering manuals; and more. Long ago, I labeled these tools Afformations—forms that say *Yes. Yes, I can learn this. Yes, I can do this. Yes, I can succeed.* Sure, off-the-shelf tools were available, but they never quite worked for me as well as my homegrown tools.

And today, I find myself applying this aspect of who I am to a volunteer endeavor. For several years, I have been a member of a nonfiction book club that meets monthly at our town library. We take turns leading the group discussion. Often the discussion revolves around the subject of the book—healthcare systems, economics of the middle class, religions and faith, neighborhoods and community, genomes and stem cells, and more. Recently, a club member asked, "How else can we talk about a book?" When some of us met recently to finalize our book selections for 2012, we started to answer that question. Here's what we did.

We looked over the various book reviews we collected when selecting the coming year's books. We flipped through the pages of *BookPage® America's Book Review* to learn how others write about books. There was nothing scientific about this approach. We spontaneously came up with items, such as genre, credibility of the author, verifiability of the data, organizational structure, voice, tone, theme, mechanics, and more. And, as the one who likes to create Afformations, it is my task now to create a tool for the club. I will type up all of the ideas from our brainstorming session, group ideas that are similar, title each group, organize the groups into a sequence that makes sense, and voilà, our nonfiction book club will have a form that says, *Yes, we can talk about the subject of our nonfiction book—and so much more.*

Someone in the group has already indicated that tools exist that provide ways to talk about nonfiction books in general and the books on our list in particular. As time goes on, we will no doubt use these resources and watch our homegrown tool evolve.

Now, tell me, what homegrown or off-the-shelf tools do you use to succeed at discussing nonfiction books or doing anything else? I would love to hear from you.

Reading Nonfiction Books

Blog posting May 23, 2015

This long weekend is a good time for me to delve into *The Path Between the Seas: The Creation of the Panama Canal 1870 – 1914* by David McCullough, this month's selection for our nonfiction book club. The book looks daunting, all 700 or so pages. Yet, what motivates me to get started is the trust I have in club members who have recommended noteworthy books by authors who can craft memorable, literary works of art.

Our method of selecting books is fairly arbitrary. If a club member likes a book and wants the club to read it, we do so as long as the roster for the year covers a variety of nonfiction genres and topics. Of the 50 plus books we have read and discussed, some have been gems.

On a long, hot, summer day, grab a drink, stretch out on a hammock, become immersed in someone else's world, and enjoy reading a great book. Ten books that I might not have selected on my own but found to be more than worthwhile might just suit you. Take a look.

10 favorite nonfiction books

Bonhoeffer: Pastor, Martyr, Prophet, Spy by Eric Metaxas. There's so much to learn about a remarkable individual who held the moral high ground, at great cost, during World War II Germany.

Destiny of the Republic: A Tale of Madness, Medicine and the Murder of a President by Candice Millard. This is a wonderful record of President Garfield's life and long, painful, mistreated illness and eventual death.

The Healing of America: A Global Quest for Better, Cheaper, and Fairer Health Care by T.S. Reid. While searching for a remedy to his own medical problem, the author uncovers how the approaches to treatment and healing vary from country to country.

The Human Age: The World Shaped By Us by Diane Ackerman. With the voice of a poet and the eye of a scientist, the author provides an optimistic look at how humans can make this a livable, sustainable world.

In the Neighborhood: The Search for Community on an American Street, One Sleepover at a Time by Peter Lovenheim. A tragedy prompted one neighbor (the author) to transform his neighborhood into a place where someone is there for you in that moment of need.

Malcolm X: Life of Reinvention by Manning Marable. Marable brought alive the life of Malcolm Little in his transformation to Malcolm X, amid all the complexity and difficulty of the American story.

The Professor and the Madman: A Tale of Murder, Insanity, and the Making of The Oxford English Dictionary by Simon Winchester. For those of us who pay attention to words and language, learning how the Oxford English Dictionary came about is fascinating. Getting to know about one prolific contributor, Dr. W. C. Minor, and his unusual home base while crafting his submissions makes for a textured, multilayered read.

Provenance: How a Con Man and a Forger Rewrote the History of Modern Art by Laney Salisbury. Though the meaning of provenance was unknown to me, I quickly learned how the art of deceptive documents can fool even the most adept and discriminating art connoisseurs.

The Snakehead: An Epic of the Chinatown Underworld and the American Dream by Patrick Radden Keefe. The smugglers spearheading the complex and precarious journey from one continent to another make for a riveting story.

Triangle: The Fire That Changed America by David von Drehle. The story of the fire in a shirtwaist factory in lower Manhattan at the turn of the 20th century reminds us that cutting corners to garner greater profit comes at great human cost.

Local authors

Our nonfiction book club typically reads some books by local authors whom we invite to participate in the discussion. Having the author right there with us to answer our questions has enriched our understanding of the book and the author's craft.

Amy Bach joined us in our discussion of *Ordinary Injustice: How America Holds Court*. Having her young son on her lap certainly added to the ambiance of our meeting.

In our discussion of *Triangle: The Fire That Changed America*, D. H. Cook, author of *Edge of the Triangle*, drew us a detailed map of the shirtwaist factory, floor by floor, window by window, door by door. We could see how grim the situation was for the many immigrant women who were at work that fateful day.

David Cay Johnston opened our eyes when discussing *The Fine Print: How Big Companies Use "Plain English" to Rob You Blind* and *Free Lunch: How the Wealthiest Americans Enrich Themselves at Government Expense (and Stick You with the Bill)*.

Peter Lovenheim was able to bring us up to date on the neighbors we met in his book, *In the Neighborhood: The Search for Community on an American Street, One Sleepover at a Time*.

Anthony J. Sciolino rounded out his story of *The Holocaust, The Church, and the Law of Unintended Consequences: How Christian Anti-Judaism Spawned Nazi Anti-Semitism*.

Your favorite books and authors

Among my 10 favorite books discussed above as well as the additional books by our community's local authors, you're sure to find some that suit you. Let me know what you liked. Recommend your favorite nonfiction books and authors. I'd love to be introduced to them, right here, right now.

Update

Our book club is still active, and I have 10 more favorites to add to the 10 selected in 2015. Keep reading.

Reading Nonfiction Books Continued

Blog posting December 7, 2021

I just circulated a list of 25 nonfiction books to book club members. At next week's meeting, we will select our books for 2022. When we do, I'll keep in mind books that have been favorites during the past five years. Take a look. You might enjoy reading them and learning from them.

10 favorite nonfiction books continued

A Woman of No Importance: The Untold Story of the American Spy Who Helped Win World War II by Sonia Purnell. Virginia Hall, an American, a spy for the British, and an amputee with only one leg, performed heroic deeds during the French resistance.

Blood in the Water: The Attica Prison Uprising of 1971 and Its Legacy by Heather Ann Thompson. With the setting for this book just an hour or so away, the events of this prison uprising were familiar from news accounts at the time. What was not familiar was the story of the devastation that occurred to real human beings and their families with lasting effects. What an eye opener.

The Elephant Company: The Inspiring Story of an Unlikely Hero and the Animals Who Helped Him Save Lives in World War II by Vicki Constantine Croke. Set in World War II Burma, elephant wallah Billy Williams put elephants to work with compassion, tenderness, and love. What the elephants accomplished building bridges and leading an escape on a mountain stairway was nothing short of miraculous.

Killers of the Flower Moon: The Osage Murders and the Birth of the FBI by David Grann. This thriller is a wake-up call of what occurs when those in power stop others they deem unworthy from rising, succeeding, and living the good life.

The Library Book by Susan Orlean. The Los Angeles Public Library burned to the ground in 1986. Library lover Susan Orlean explores why, who, and how this happened. From the devastation through the rebuilding and beyond, the library's role as a magnet for people from all walks of life comes alive. There are many people to thank for making the public library a special place. I, for one, couldn't live without it.

Say Nothing: A True Story of Murder and Memory in Northern Ireland by Patrick Radden Keefe. Understanding the opposing parties during The Troubles in Northern Ireland, where violence ruled, is no easy matter. Patrick Radden Keefe gives an up close and personal account of a 1972 murder and exposes the personalities and motivations of the time.

Seven Million: A Cop, a Priest, a Soldier for the IRA, and the Still-Unsolved Rochester Brink's Heist by Gary Craig. A local reporter and local crime story, the names and places were very familiar to book club members. With $7 million yet unfound and a tie to The Troubles in Northern Ireland, this book was a winner for our book club.

Strangers in Their Own Land: Anger and Mourning on the American Right by Arlie Russell Hochschild. For me, the highlight of this book was how Arlie Russell Hochschild synthesized what she learned about one side of America into one Deep Story and what she knew about the other side into another Deep Story. Different narratives. Different worldviews. The challenge is how to cross the divide.

These Truths: A History of the United States by Jill LePore. What I loved about this dense book that starts in 1492 and goes to just a few years' short of the present day is the message I received: knowing our history is critical to understanding and confronting present times.

The Warmth of Other Suns: The Epic Story of America's Great Migration by Isabel Wilkerson. Isabel Wilkerson tells the stories of real families who migrated from the South to the North and West in search of a better life. For black Americans, *better* was far from perfect. Captivated by the beautiful writing and rich, thoroughly researched content, our book club is now reading Wilkerson's second book, *Caste: The Origins of Our Discontents*. Even in the opening pages, it's clear that *Caste* is another must-read book.

Book Club Prep

Blog posting February 26, 2017

Are you a member of a book club? If so, you may
wonder if your book club is representative of the
many, many book clubs that thrive in so many venues
and so many communities throughout the U.S. and the
world. If you are not yet fortunate enough to be part of
a book club, you might have wondered what exactly
occurs.

To book club members who are curious about other
clubs, to book club wannabes, and, especially, to
members of a nonfiction book club I'm attending
tomorrow, here's a sneak preview of what to expect.

Our book club protocol

In our book club, members arrive promptly, since the
room typically is full with 20 or so serious readers
gathered around a large conference table in our town's
library. Club membership is exclusive, only in the
sense that we are serious readers. We each attend
voluntarily and welcome whoever walks in the door.
Often first-timers become regulars.

We select our books for the coming year in December,
and, at each month's meeting, the library provides
copies of the book for the following month, which we
check out and begin to read. Club members take turns
leading the discussion and do so willingly (or with a
gentle nudge). Each month's leader brings a unique,
personal style to the table. What all share is a

commitment to creating an atmosphere that is respectful. We talk and we listen. We explore many facets of a book and we learn.

Our book for this month is *The Botany of Desire: A Plant's-Eye View of the World* by Michael Pollan. It will be my pleasure (truly!) to lead tomorrow's discussion, since I loved, loved, loved this book.

Here's what I have in mind:

> Greet everyone who walks through the door—the regulars and the newbies. Be sure that everyone has a nametag, a copy of the year's schedule, and "Talking About Nonfiction Books"—a discussion sheet that club members assembled over time.
>
> Kick off the discussion with a brief introduction (my name, length of time with the book club, interests, and so forth) and ask others to do the same. As part of their introductions, ask them to share a few aspects of the book that they want to discuss.
>
> With pencil (yes, always a pencil with an eraser) in hand, I circle items on the discussion sheet that we should cover during our time together and scribble notes. For me, this sheet, with everyone's input noted, guides the give-and-take that ensues.
>
> I then let people talk. Let them ask. Let them discuss. Let them argue (amicably). The task is to simply herd the cats.

My two cents

Every now and then, I throw in my two cents.

Related to the author, Michael Pollan, did I find his plant's-eye view of the world credible? Yes. The many sources referenced in the book, both primary and secondary, tell me that he learned an enormous amount in order to write:

> Chapter 1 Desire: Sweetness / Plant: The Apple

> Chapter 2 Desire: Beauty / Plant: The Tulip

> Chapter 3 Desire: Intoxication / Plant: Marijuana

> Chapter 4 Desire: Control / The Potato

Beyond the research, Pollan himself is a gardener who digs in and gets his hands messy. In *The Botany of Desire: A Plant's-Eye View of the World*, he has unearthed truths about the co-evolution of plants and humans.

What I most loved about the book was the artistry in which Pollan plied his craft. The language, the metaphors, the meanderings made this a joyful read.

The discussion sheet asks, "Would you read other books on the subject, by this author, in this genre?" Yes, yes, yes.

At some point, I will ask, "If you were to write Chapter 5, what desire and plant would you add?"

Tomorrow

Our discussion tomorrow will be open to a variety of voices, which is sure to enrich the human crop gathered at the table. I can hardly wait.

Your turn...

Tell us about your book club. Where do you meet? What do your read? Who attends? What is the best part for you—reading, discussing, something else?

Update

Courtesy of that nasty, unwelcome virus, from March 2020 through June 2021, our book club met via Zoom. Imperfect as gathering remotely was, the wonders of technology enabled us to keep the club intact. Now that we are back at the library, we have moved to a larger room and for the most part, stay masked and distanced and happy to see each other's twinkling eyes.

Passages

Gratitude. Generosity. Sustenance.

Blog posting May 25, 2014

Next weekend, I am attending my high school reunion. Many, many years have passed—more than I care to admit. I will be driving a relatively short distance, just 70 miles or so, to the place I forever consider my home and will be staying in the bedroom I shared—from kindergarten through high school—with an older sister. At just about the same time, we both moved to new digs. She got married, and I went to college. Until recently, my mother (Ma) lived upstairs, along with one of my three brothers, and other members of our family have occupied the downstairs. With Ma now playing "Pennies from Heaven" and other favorite songs on a piano in her celestial abode, returning home is no longer the same, but with family there, it is still very, very good.

For me, this upcoming trip requires no extensive travel arrangements, and I'm all set as far as attire, since that is not a primary concern. For any occasion, including this one, I simply put myself together and am presentable. After a glance in the mirror to adjust anything that might obviously be amiss, I move on.

Yet, this occasion, this milestone, this high school reunion does cause me to pause.

Gratitude

I think with gratitude about the preparation that so many classmates have put into this event. Gary got the ball rolling and has kept it moving, encouraging and cajoling us to attend this gathering and to find and invite others, wherever they may have landed. Mary recruited her daughter to compile and post a contact list, which seemed to grow day by day. Didi created a website, with then and now pictures and stories. Janie and Bonnie collected funds to donate to our high school, which, like most schools today, can use financial help. Sara arranged a dinner in advance of the reunion. Alex started us thinking about the too-long list of classmates who are no longer living. He will make sure that they are remembered. Others have done their part to prepare a reunion that will be both meaningful and fun.

Generosity

I think of how each of us has matured since those long-ago high school days. By now, we have learned a thing or two about life and what matters. We surely have something of value to offer to make this reunion a joyous occasion. Listen to the classmate you once overlooked. Say those kind words to someone who needs to hear them. Whatever arises, be of help and be of good cheer. With the many accomplishments of this fortunate class, be ready and willing to share and to give. Find a way to demonstrate your gratitude to the reunion planners—and those in attendance—with your own expression of generosity. I recently heard how at one reunion, each table had a form with trivia questions to involve guests who accompanied classmates and to keep the conversation lively. That's something I can easily create and will do so this week.

Sustenance

I think of takeaways from this reunion. Sure, there will be photos, but there should be something more, something good, something that sustains each of us when we think back on this reunion. When I have that extra something in hand, in mind, and in heart, I'll truly have more to write.

A Granddaughter Remembers

Blog posting April 16, 2013

In early 2013, while reading "Shifra's Story," written by my book club colleague, I recalled writing some of Kalman's story and discovered my handwritten pages, likely written around 1980. This story is my recollection of how my grandfather, my Pa, started a journey at the turn of the 20th century from Must, Poland, that led him, eventually, to the United States. With the passing during the last days of 2012 of Pa's precious daughter, who was my dear mother, I treasure the many family stories that live in my memory. I will do my part now to preserve them by writing what I consider to be sacred texts.

"Mmmm. Ouch. Ugh." moaned Kalman. His little legs ached as he ran. His little arms hurt as they held on to the wagon. Running—literally—to freedom and safety meant holding on to the back of the eggman's horse-drawn wagon and keeping up with a horse's four legs that were much longer and speedier than his two.

"What's that I hear?" murmured Reb Mayer. He stopped the wagon. "Who's there?" Reb Mayer stopped the wagon, sprung to the ground, walked to the back of the wagon, and found Kalman. "What are you doing here?"

No answer came from the eight-year-old boy. A pleading, pained look said, "Please offer me a ride."

"Come on up front. Have a crust of bread. And tell me why you're here."

Kalman began, "I know you stop at Bialystock. I want to go there." To Kalman, Bialystock meant Mama Gittel's sister and her children. It meant an end to Must.

For Kalman, his Must home after his mother's death and his father's remarriage was just a place—and not a pleasant, safe, or happy one. It meant food locked in cupboards, hunger, and harsh words from a mean stepmother who told lies of misbehavior to Kalman's father when he returned from his logging trips— making rafts and rowing them to the other side of Must's river—resulting in painful, humiliating, unjust beatings. Must meant ridicule from children who had coins to a buy a bagel after Kader when Kalman could not.

Must, too, meant a beginning of self-reliance— collecting and filling his pockets full of feathers during the seasons of grass-covered ground and small metals during the seasons of snow-covered ground— and exchanging both feathers and metals for kopecks from a neighboring lady. Kopecks enabled Kalman to enjoy an after-Kader treat, like the other boys, eliminating their taunts. But they did nothing to save him from his stepmother, no substitute for his own warm, gentle, kind Mama Gittel. Now sitting up front in the wagon with the eggman, Kalman wanted to find his aunt.

On this wagon, heading away from pain, moving in a new direction, Kalman had already come so far. He had made his preparations. Earlier, he had thought,

"I know Reb Mayer delivers eggs to Bialystock. I can ask him to take me there. Yet, he will surely ask her for permission, which will cause me even greater trouble. Or, he will ask him, which will also mean pain. Neither my stepmother nor my father will ever allow me to leave. So, I won't ask. I'll just go."

Kalman carefully watched the eggman make his deliveries. He learned the route and knew the last stop before leaving Must.

On this particular day, eager and in wait behind a tree, with no one in sight, Kalman watched the eggman make his final stop in Must. Then he ran behind the wagon, expecting to hop on board the back of the wagon and ride. His little arms grabbed hold, but his little legs just couldn't make the climb. So Kalman just ran and ran, holding on for dear life.

Now, how good it felt to sit up front and to eat. The small comforts of life maybe yet would be his.

"Kalman, what will I do with you in Bialystock?" asked Reb Mayer, amazed that so young and gentle a child had so much persistence, courage, and desire.

"Just take me to my aunt. Like my real mother, she has red hair."

"I know only one woman in Bialystock who has red hair. I will take you to her."

And so they rode, with Kalman dreaming of a new life. In Bialystock, Reb Mayer drove the wagon here and there, delivering eggs. In the center of one town square, he stopped his wagon and pointed to a house, "The lady with red hair lives there." Kalman jumped off the wagon and looked up at the house. In a window, holding an infant, was a woman with red hair. She spotted him and recognized that this was Sister Gittel's Kalman, now her Kalman. She welcomed him into his new home.

What family treasures, alive in your memory, are you preserving? What are your sacred texts?

Update

My new-found cousin Rachelle, the granddaughter of Kalman's brother Harris, has helped piece together who was who. With her dogged persistence, the story of our common heritage has begun to unfold.

Kalman, my handsome grandfather as a young man, is in the back row center. He is with his siblings—Becky (back row, left), Reva (back row, right), Goldie (front row, left), and Harris (front row, right)—and their father, my great-grandfather Lewis.

Give Away that Which You Hope to Receive

Blog posting June 26, 2012

At a recent memorial service, I said a final good-bye to Hannah. An artist, she taught ceramics in her home studio for many years. I recalled what I saw then—incredible patience, tolerance, and joy as her students selected a statue, a jar, an ornament; colors; and textures. Some of her students excelled, winning numerous awards. Others created imperfect pieces that continue to adorn many, many homes, including my own. At the service, what I most recalled about Hannah in her studio was the atmosphere she created. She allowed all—the young, old, talented, struggling, talkative, silent, compulsive, confused—to be, to do, and to create what was possible for them.

I thought about Hannah during a workshop last week in which a group of participants worked through some of the activities in *Career Success in 12 Easy Steps: A Journal.* We explored the question, "What types of obstacles do you face on your road to success?" The conversation focused on getting others to see us as a whole person, a human being who is capable, qualified, and well-equipped to do the task. Hannah was a pro at seeing and encouraging others.

True, if we want others to see us favorably, we need to do our part to influence and evoke a favorable impression by demonstrating and conveying our value and worth. Yet the only impression we control is the one we make in our own minds and hearts.

So, let us not become an obstacle to others' success. We can start by seeing others as they are and could yet become. Let us look beyond our own projections and prejudices and do our part to understand and value those with whom we interact. Let us see their abilities, their competencies, their strengths, their achievements, and their potential. Let us provide opportunities for other human beings—flawed and imperfect as they are—to grow and thrive. After all, is that not what we want for ourselves?

Life is funny. We must be willing to give away that which we hope to receive.

Dear One

Blog posting July 31, 2016

Within every tradition and every culture, rites of passage occur. Here are some words I shared recently at such an occasion, a wonderful time to pause and reflect.

Snapshots

Dear One, in my mind's eye, I see you... Sitting on a little chair and listening attentively to your beloved Great Grandma G playing her piano. Often helping Great Grandma G find her walking cane so lovingly, so compassionately. Selling lemonade and cookies to passersby going to and from ballgames, charming all. Conducting a seder (ceremonial meal) with great competence and poise.

This family is very proud of you and love you dearly.

Your family past

Some in your family are no longer here, but we remember them.

I recall how your Great Grandpa B tidied up your Great Grandma H's studio before and after every class. In these classes, your Great Grandma H created a healing atmosphere, showing great patience to all.

Your Great Grandpa S was up at the crack of dawn every morning, working each day to provide for his large family. He returned home from work with big bags of groceries to keep his family, and others welcomed into the house, well fed and well cared-for. Your Great Grandma G, as you well know, showered all who knew her with wit, wisdom, and music.

We remember your mom's parents and your Uncle R, who recently passed away.

Your family present

Dear One, look around you, and you'll see so many who love you. Your grandparents are guiding you to become what we call a *mensch* (a person of integrity and honor). You can learn a lot from them. They are devoted to each other, to their siblings, to their children, and to each of their grandchildren.

Your mom and your dad are here for you in every way. They want the best for you. We thank them and all who are congregated here today for supporting, teaching, and loving you.

You are our future

And now, Dear One, you have a job to do. Please continue to learn, to mature, and to develop into a contributing, responsible young woman. Do your part to make this community and this world better and brighter. Do so willingly, happily, and joyfully.

Now, let's celebrate this wonderful day.

I'll See You Again

Blog posting January 10, 2013

Having my wonderful mother for so many years has been an immeasurable blessing. A source of love, encouragement, joy, and inspiration, she passed away on December 27, 2012. She is—and ever will be—in my heart. I would like to share her with you through my tribute at her memorial service on December 30, 2012.

"Judy, you talk to them." This is what my Ma would say to me when she was occupied. And so I will share what I believe Ma would say, because these are sentiments she has conveyed over many years.

Sandra dear, you know how to cook everything just the way I like it. If Judy decides to cook, tell her exactly what to do. You and Mike and the grandchildren and great-grandchildren you raised gave me enormous, constant joy. Dawn, Dave, and Steve have been my protectors from the time they were very young. I am so grateful. Please take care of your sister and brothers.

Judy dear, my next born, you have been my angel, my peaceful joy. You have gone through everything with me. G-d will richly bless you in His way for your devotion.

Bobby dear, I am so very proud of you, for the professional man you became. For every family occasion, you were here—with pies and cookies and treats. Keep up your running and take good care of Miss Callie.

Larry dear, what can I say? You adapted our home to meet my every need, from marking the octaves on my piano to adding railings to the stairway to making beautiful furniture. You made it possible for me to thrive at home. You have been a rock—to me and to our whole family. Please keep up your mountain hiking. And make some clocks. Maxine will help you sell them.

Richie dear, my precious baby. You were my superman, flying down the street in your cape, a towel tied around your neck. You opened every jar, using your superhuman strength! And you have continued to be a strong, yet gentle, compassionate, kind, wonderful son. I love you and Meg and my handsome, talented grandsons, Sam and Jake. They will be big shots one day.

And my wonderful nieces and nephews—Shirley, Maxine, Marty, Suzi, Gerry, Janet, and Syd—I have loved you as I have loved my own and am ever grateful for your special gifts.

There are so many others to thank for a wonderful life and now to comfort. You know who you are. Please be there for one another. I'll see you again.

Her Company

About Us

This writing is part of our website easescommunications.com.

Our clients' organizational cultures often include shortened product life cycles, reengineered processes, reorganization, expansion, and flux. We remain mindful of the culture's impact on those with whom we interact. Guided by the principle that our clients' success is our success, we keep pace with global technologies and trends, ever mindful of how our solutions secure a competitive edge for our clients.

We expect that our efforts will result in cultivating satisfied clients who will continue to use our services and recommend them to others anywhere in the world. We approach our work with order and maturity, with cooperation and respect. The result? Long-time clients who value our work and our workers.

Our company

Who knew when Judy Shenouda accepted a technical writing assignment many years ago that a thriving business would emerge? The year was 1985, and Judy was working in a university's career services office where jobs often came in for job seekers. Judy's colleague received a request for a technical writer and handed it to Judy. "You can do this. Give the guy a call." Judy did so, spent four months writing a policy and procedure manual for the largest employer in the area, and continued taking on contract writing assignments. When the volume of work exceeded her own time and energy, she found others to help—some of whom are with her to this day. With them, she built a business and a reputation for delivering quality work.

Judy and her team continue to answer the call. They provide first-rate solutions to clients' documentation challenges. Without fuss or fanfare, they simply—and happily—get the job done.

Let Shenouda support your projects

- Writers and editors

- Instructional designers

- Project managers

- Localization specialists

- Web developers

- IT support

Contractors. Freelancers. Human Resources. Personnel. Supplemental Workforce. Temporary Help. Virtual Workers.

Whatever term you use, the right people are key.

Our owner

Judith Ellison Shenouda is owner of Shenouda Associates Inc., a business that researches, writes, and edits the many professional publications that streamline processes, launch products, and promote each client's brand. Our owner is a networker  extraordinaire. At the hub of a thriving network of professional associates, Judy believes that networking comes down to connecting with others in a meaningful way.

Judy is an active member of the professional communication community and a frequent presenter at local, national, and international conferences. A seasoned educator and communicator, she

- Remembers faces, names, and conversations

- Offers assistance, provides encouragement, and applauds efforts and successes

- Cares about others and introduces them to those who can benefit from the introduction

Judy makes it a priority to connect with the next generation of workers, recognizing their rich potential and capabilities using new media as modes of communication. At the same time, she applauds the technical acumen, product knowledge, facility with many publishing tools, and sound judgment of experienced workers.

Education

- **State University of New York at Buffalo**
Bachelor of Arts degree in English and
Secondary Education

- **S.I. Newhouse School of Public
Communications at Syracuse University**
Master of Arts degree in Literacy Journalism

- Additional courses in curriculum design and
development, group dynamics, information
studies, publication management, and project
management

Author

- *Career Success in 12 Easy Steps: A Journal*
(https://www.amazon.com/Career-Success-12-
Easy-Steps/dp/1732222312/)

- *A Bisl of This, A Bisl of That: Eating Our Way*
(https://www.amazon.com/Bisl-This-That-
Eating-Our/dp/1732222320/)

- *Living Well in Froggy's World of Plenty: Sweet Talk
to Read Aloud*
(https://www.amazon.com/Living-Well-
Froggys-World-Plenty/dp/1732222304/)

- *A Step, a Stroll, a Blog, a Book: Collecting My
Thoughts* (https://www.amazon.com/Step-
Stroll-Blog-Book-Collecting/dp/B09PKQSZBM)

Our clients

Our clients vary in size and industry.

- Consultants, small businesses, and multinational corporations

- Not-for-private, public, and private entities

- Service providers, software developers, and hardware manufacturers

- Healthcare, human services, education, publishing, legal, and industrial markets

All have a commitment to excellence, which we definitely share.

Your advantage

When we develop your communication products, both those intended to support the products that you sell and service as well as those intended to support your business processes, expect the best to occur:

- Your projects proceed smoothly.

- Your work gets done on time, on budget, and according to your specifications.

- Your team is enhanced with new, creative perspectives.

- You and your team have the time to do what you do best.

- Customers purchase your products and use your services.

- Your business remains competitive and profitable in a global marketplace.

Closing

A Step, a Stroll, a Blog, a Book: Collecting My Thoughts wraps up a decade of blog postings. The years from 2011 through 2021 proved to be productive ones for this business owner and business, for this author and independent publisher.

This book might be finished, but our work continues. Reach out with your questions and comments, and with your authoring, publishing, and business needs.

Judith Ellison Shenouda

Email me at Shenouda@easescommunication.com.

Read my blog at judithshenouda.wordpress.com.

Visit my author page at www.amazon.com/Judith-Ellison-Shenouda/e/B07KFN96DZ.

Visit our website at easescommunications.com.

Notes

Made in the USA
Middletown, DE
22 February 2022

61548552R00066